GET OVER YOURSELF

BY

MARCELLUS ROBERTS II

Edited by
Carolyn Richards
Cre8ivly.com
Hello@cre8ivly.com

TABLE OF CONTENTS

ACKNOWLEDGEMENTS

For those who are reading these words right now, I just want to say thank you! This book is really a big moment for me in my life. To be able to share this moment with you means everything to me. Most would think since I love to read books, and have written one now too, that I have loved reading my whole life. To them, I would have to say they are wrong. I HATED reading growing up. Accelerated Reading was my greatest enemy in grade school. But to now have a book out of my very own, one that I put a lot of care, insight and experience into, really does make the younger version of me proud. I have to thank my lil sister Zoe and lil brother Zephania for always being My Why! I must thank my Dad for being the greatest teacher and supporter in my life. There is so much I have learned from them. I love them with my entire heart. I want to say thank you to my friends and extended family that have been there for me in the past in ways I am forever grateful for. I would like to thank people who have exited my life in any fashion. Even if we don't talk anymore, the memories and experiences are a part of our lives; and we

shared that. Most of all, I want to thank YOU

for taking the time to read this!

Please do enjoy this book. I've written it to be

a short and simple read. Read it again. Then

the next time you read it, highlight it. Write

in it. Make it a journal. My vision for this

book is to add tremendous value to YOU.

Your feedback would be greatly appreciated!

CHAPTER 1: INTRODUCTION

If you let it, this step-by-step plan will change your life. Many times, along my journey I wanted to quit, and you probably will too; but on the other side is clarity and awareness that will create everlasting change.

Earl Nightingale's definition of success is the progressive realization of a worthy goal or ideal. So, let me ask you this: "What is stopping you from being successful? Who stopped you from pursuing your passion or your dreams? What excuses do you have for not being fulfilled by what you do?" Maybe it was your ex-spouse who broke your heart and put you through turmoil that has been difficult to recover from. Maybe it's your boss scheduling you for SOOO many hours you don't have time to yourself to work on things you are passionate about. Maybe you're a parent and the kiddos are constantly seeking your attention, making it difficult to concentrate on your goals. Oh, you said you *don't have money* to pursue your ideas, so you don't try at all; I see. Do you believe the world is against you; and that is why you can't catch a break? I've personally been there. I'll tell you like this. Chances are, *you* are stopping you from being successful. *You* are stopping you from pursuing your passion and your dreams. You probably know this already; but it is much easier to pass blame to someone or something else.

I strongly believe that if you take to heart everything you will learn in this short book, you will GET OVER YOURSELF. You will possess the ability to always operate at your maximum potential regardless of the situation or circumstances that may stand in your way. Regardless of gender, race,

religion, it doesn't matter who you are; if you

<u>actively implement</u> these concepts, you will

GET OVER YOURSELF.

You will learn the importance of

figuring out your why and what that does to

guide you to your purpose in life. You will

learn how to build your very own values

based on your why; so that you don't have to

adopt other's beliefs. You will learn how to

create standards based on your why; the

non-negotiables, in your life to hold yourself,

others and your environment accountable. Of

course, making all of these changes about

yourself will feel uncomfortable. That is good and expected. You will learn how to act in the face of our greatest oppressor, Fear. When you implement all these things into your life, I promise you will step out of your own way and GET OVER YOURSELF.

You are probably asking yourself, what does this guy know about standards and values, purpose in life and how to get over fear. In college I lost my way and sense of identity when I decided to hang up the cleats in 2017 as a student-athlete. Up to that point I lived up to other people's expectations and found that it was driving me insane. I did not know what I was truly interested in or what I truly wanted to pursue in life. I did things during my time in school like partying, drinking, and sleeping around a lot. None, absolutely none of these things brought me value because I was still miserable inside. I blamed others and my circumstances for my confusion in life. All I had to do was look in the mirror to find the culprit of all my problems. Once I decided that I was the problem, I soon came to realize that I could solve those problems as well. Through much effort and time spent working on myself and raising the bar for how I lived and carried myself, I noticed life became more fulfilling. Although life was still throwing many punches at me, I could now maneuver and still come out on top every single time. People that I thought had my best interest in mind revealed their true colors. My newfound values and standards exceeded their perception of who I was. As I allowed them to fall out of my life, I began to excel and grow even further. This book is not something to take lightly. This book will be the difference between living for yourself and your purpose versus living for others. Your transformation will not happen overnight;

but I promise, it is a journey worth taking. Let

us begin the process on how to GET OVER

YOURSELF!

CHAPTER 2: THE WHY

WHAT IS PURPOSE?

The first step to GET OVER YOURSELF would be to find out your why. Essentially, your why is your purpose for doing whatever it is that you seek to pursue. For instance, my why or my purpose for writing this book is to positively impact people by sharing the process I took to GET OVER MYSELF. Finding out your why gives meaning to your life. Many think their why or purpose in life are the gifts they were "born" with; but I believe that is only a part of it. Yes, some of us are born with more natural talent in different areas of our life; but our connectivity to others, our environment, and the world we live in is what truly makes us different. Really, purpose or the why, are the meaningful things we live for in life; and throughout life, they can change!

WHAT LIFE IS LIKE WITHOUT IT

Have you ever gone through a midlife crisis or a moment where you felt purposeless? I have plenty of time; most significantly when I made the decision to move on from sports in college. Some of these moments may come after a bad break-up, leaving or being let go from a job you built tenure at, or even failed goals that you invested much time into. We have all been there. The thing I noticed the most when looking back at all those experiences was realizing how lonely I felt in those moments. I felt disconnected from the world and reality. I recall how I felt my confidence and self-esteem plummet to lows I never knew existed. Subsequently, I had an epiphany.

Certainly, if we can reach such lows in life,

that must mean we can reach unimaginable

highs as well. So, I knew there was a way to

dig myself out of the hole I was in.

HOW I FOUND MY WHY

Back then in 2017 and on, I did not

realize what I had done to dig myself out of

the lows I created for myself. Upon

reflection, I see now that I first figured out

what was most meaningful in my life to live

for. I no longer lived for others through

sports and their perception of my athletic

abilities. I concluded that I could move on in life without it. It was late in the season when I made the decision to stop playing football. Ironically, when I made that decision, I had the best game possible during one of my worst performing seasons in my entire athletic career. This gave me the confirmation I needed about my decision to move on. What led to me making this decision was asking myself a series of questions as to why I was even playing and pursuing football in the first place.

I never aspired to play in the NFL. Knowing the short careers most players have at that caliber of the game I wondered what I was playing for. I realized I was really only playing to increase my odds of gaining a scholarship to get my education paid for. I asked myself "Why do I want to get my schooling paid for?" I thought about the fact that I grew up in a household where neither of my parents went to nor graduated from college. So, if my parents didn't go to college, why did I feel it was so important for me to do. I have always been a great learner; but I hated school. Then I realized I was going to school to be a positive example for my little brother and sister. This realization struck what felt like lightning through my core. I soon came to realize the real reason I was in this position in the first place. I wasn't playing football for the passion of the game. My real reason for playing was a deeper means to accomplish a goal that surpassed my actual love for the game. I didn't realize what I was doing when I was asking myself all these questions. It wasn't until 2019 when a mentor of mine shared an exercise with myself and others that I discovered the answer. Anyone can do this exercise to define the meaningful purpose they have in life. This exercise will also lead us to building our very own Values. So, make sure you do not skip this exercise.

EXERCISE: 7 LEVELS DEEP

The 7 Levels Deep exercise is a technique most popularized by Dean Graziosi that helps to discover the real meaning and purpose in our lives and in what we do. The best part about it is that anyone can do it and you will probably learn more about yourself than you did before. To start this exercise, I'd recommend getting a piece of paper out or a journal, if you are into that and putting at the top "My Why". First, ask yourself "What is it that you want to do?" This could be in a specific area in your life or what you want to do for a living. We will talk about how it is okay to Change Your Mind in a later chapter. So, this can change down the line. Then ask yourself, "Why is that important to you?" Once you have figured that out, do it again. Then again. And again. Until you have taken it to a minimum of 7 Levels Deep. The reason why you want to take this line of questioning a minimum of 7 Levels Deep is because the first few levels are very superficial. Those levels will not be deep enough to hold you accountable to the purpose you want to live

for. For example, one might say "They want

more money in their life". Then I would ask,

"Why is it important to you to have more

money?". Typical responses would be that

they want to be rich and or wealthy. Then my

response would be "Okay so why is it

important to be rich or wealthy?". Then they

might say that "Growing up their family was

poor". Then once again, "Why is it important

to you to not be poor?". They might say "It

was hard growing up seeing their parents

struggle to provide for the family". Then

again, "Why is it important to you to not see

your parents struggle or have difficulty providing for the family?". They might respond saying that "They wish they knew more about how to create income to help their parents and family; but they didn't". Again, "Why is it important to know how to create income?". They might say "Their parents wouldn't have had to stress so much about money and spend their entire lives working for it". One more time, "Why is it important to you to not stress about money and not spend your life working for it?". One might say that "If they have to constantly stress over working for money to survive, they will miss out on living life to its fullest".

So now we can clearly see the reason why this person wants more money. It is not just to be rich or to just have money for the sake of having it. They know deep down that if they do not possess the skills to create their own income, they will live lives like their parents. They will constantly live-in survival mode. They will constantly stress about not having money. Performing this exercise and delving into deeper levels will keep you accountable to the things you find meaningful in life, your purpose, your why.

CHAPTER 3: VALUES

WHAT ARE VALUES?

Now that we have established what gives meaning to our life, we can move on to the second step to GET OVER YOURSELF and start to build our very own values. First, we should define what values are and what they do in our life. From what I have gathered, simply put, values are the beliefs we find to be important in our life. For instance, some things that I value would be integrity, education, self-love, family and so on. It's no secret that we adopt beliefs from others from what we are taught and what we are influenced by. What I have seen in others and also in myself, is that when we do things against our values, often we regret our decisions. Even if we didn't have pre-existing awareness of our values, our gut or intuition always told us to do otherwise in those moments. Can you think of a time when you were doing something or you were with someone, and your gut told you that you shouldn't? Chances are you were going against your values. Before I show you how I found my own values and how you can do so for yourself, we should take a look at some of the different types of values you can build.

TYPES OF VALUES

There are many different ways to look at values. Personally, I like to keep it simple. In my eyes you can break up values into three different categories. You can look at personal values, work values, and character values. When it comes to personal values these are the things you believe that guide you to happiness and fulfillment. Some examples of these could be your religious or spiritual connection, family, education, etc. Your work values are going to be the beliefs that guide you to fulfillment in your job or career. Some examples of these could be flexibility, hands-on activities, innovation, etc. Lastly, your character values will be your beliefs that make you a decent human being. Some examples of this could be integrity, authenticity, self-love, etc. You can break up the categories of your values into many ways and as deep as you'd like. However, I've always found that simplicity is the best way.

Now let's look at how I found my Values and how you can do the same.

HOW I FOUND MY VALUES

So, after I found my why, or the things that give meaning to my life, I started to notice that I felt out of place in many different situations. There was one time when I was at a party. It was really late. To be completely honest, while I was there, I felt like I didn't belong. Before figuring out my why I had been to plenty of parties at all times of the day and night, so this was no abnormality. I was thinking to myself, "What am I doing here? Why do I feel this way? I don't want to be here..."

It was almost like a higher power within me was telling me that I didn't belong, or I was going against myself. Afterwards, slowly but surely, I wasn't going to parties anymore. Additionally, I stopped sleeping around with many women. For a period of time, I stopped smoking and drinking in my leisure time, because it started to feel like a waste of time. I started to notice I was not putting myself in positions or making choices that went against my why. Suddenly it clicked that my values had changed! Here is how you can change yours as well.

EXERCISE: MY NEW VALUES

If you have not done the first exercise, 7 Levels Deep, then this exercise will be more difficult to do. So, I highly encourage you to complete the 7 Levels Deep exercise before going any further. If you must, go ahead and pull that same sheet of paper out. If you would like, pull out another page to write your values on. You can title this "My New Values". Now write down those three categories, personal, work, and character while also leaving some room under each section. I would also write the definitions of each category as well just to give yourself guidance. Now all you must do is describe what values you could build or now have based off of your why; or the things that give meaning to your life. Going back to our previous example in the 7 Levels Deep exercise, we could say that this person values financial literacy as a personal belief. We could also say for work they might value a work-life balance. For character they might value growth or being knowledgeable. So, what are your new values? Now that you

have established those, we can now solidify

our standards for ourselves and others.

CHAPTER 4: STANDARDS

WHAT ARE STANDARDS?

Now that we have figured out what the meaningful things in our life are and also how that correlates with our values, we can talk about our standards. Standards can be defined as absolute, inalienable laws that you set not only for yourself but for others as well. These will be your non-negotiables. Either others or you must meet the bare minimum when it comes to the standards.

For example, if I were to ever sell anything, I would expect myself to give more value than what I ask in return. This is a law for me. And I would never subject myself to anything less. Standards keep us accountable in times when others will infringe upon what we believe, or our values. Where the real power lies in having standards is when we are the ones who resist putting ourselves in positions to infringe upon what we believe. This is self-accountability. No matter what's going on, what is offered or what may come as a result, if it does not meet the expectations of our values, then we have no business lowering our standards by participating in that opportunity.

CONFORMITY

What I found myself doing in many situations when I didn't understand what was meaningful in my life or when I was living up to other peoples' beliefs and expectations, is that I was conforming to a way of living that I did not like. This is not only what I saw in myself but what I grew to see in many other people in this world. When I see people that conform to what they think is normal or what everyone else is doing it tells me that they don't think for themselves. It tells me that they don't have a set of values that they came up with on their own. It tells me they live for other people's beliefs. It shows me that they are contemptuous with how things are going, regardless of whether they like or dislike the lifestyle and the results that it brings. I believe this because this is what I saw within myself.

We are heavily influenced by our environment. Sometimes we conform to the wrong path. We never realize it until something fills us with regret; often when it is too late. When you make decisions and operate in alignment with your standards, regardless of whether the outcome or result is what you are looking for or not, you know that you are doing what is in your best interest. So, you won't be filled with regret. Therefore, conformity is dangerous because there is no sense of self accountability. It's very easy to pass the blame onto others or our circumstances rather than acknowledging the fault in ourselves for not thinking on our own.

HOW I FOUND MY STANDARDS

I started to notice that because of me living in accordance with my values, certain things and people were falling in and out of my life. I felt more confident about myself and the decisions I was making. Even if the right decision led to me being unhappy, I knew that it was in my best interest to follow through on whatever I was doing. I felt like I had direction because I had a plan of action and I executed on it consistently. Certain people that I thought were my closest friends and peers exited my life because they felt

threatened by my newfound standards and

values. My values became in direct

correlation with how I carried myself and

what I allowed and didn't allow access to in

my life. Instead of waiting for life to change

for me, I became the change that I wanted to

see in my life. I became the dictator of what I

allowed to have power over me and what I

didn't allow. I could say no without any

reservation. I knew that whatever

opportunity presented itself, if I had to say no

to it, then it wasn't in direct correlation with

my new values or new standards that I held myself to.

EXERCISE: RAISING THE BAR

Once again, if you haven't completed the last exercise please do so before you move on to this one. I call this exercise "Raising the Bar" because you are going to raise the bar that you hold yourself accountable to by creating new standards. Very similar to the last exercise, what you are going to do is take a look at the values that you wrote down to help see what standards you can create. Personally, I found that one of my values was not being afraid to take risks. So as a standard, I told myself I would not waiver in the face of adversity. Let's go back to the example that we used earlier about the person who wanted more money. Perhaps one of their values is financial literacy. Therefore, a standard could be to educate themselves on economics and surround themselves with others who are like-minded.

Remember, the most important thing about this exercise is to align your standards with your values. It will be your beliefs that will hold you accountable more than anything or anybody else can. This type of self-accountability will make you stronger as an individual. It doesn't necessarily matter the number; it matters the quality of the standards and whether you see yourself holding yourself accountable to them. Now that we have figured out our why, and we've built new values and new standards for ourselves, based off of our why; you can best believe that you will feel uncomfortable during this process. Therefore, in order to operate at our maximum potential and press beyond feeling uncomfortable we must discuss fear.

CHAPTER 5: FEAR

WHAT IS FEAR?

I believe that it is reasonable to say that after making all these changes, that fear would arise as a result. However, before we go any further with this ideal, we should identify what fear really is. While I am no scientist nor an expert regarding the brain, to my understanding it has three main functions. One, the brain collects and stores memories. Two, it regulates all our bodily functions. Lastly, three, it tends to magnify

risk. Risk essentially is anything the brain is

not used to. Therefore, when we do

something for the first time it seems to be

the hardest thing to do in our life; but

afterwards it doesn't seem as bad as we first

thought it to be. Do you remember your first

time behind the wheel of a car? Do you

remember your first time riding a bike? What

about your first kiss; that was nerve-wracking

huh? Maybe after the first exposure or a few

exposures, that initial fear went away.

This is what I like to refer to as our

comfort zone. I will go into a little more detail

about this in the next chapter but stepping out of our comfort zone will send a signal to our brain to magnify the risk! Since we are very habitual beings, we store and collect a lot of habits within our comfort zone and those include our behaviors as well. So, expect to feel fear when opportunities present themselves and you have a chance to implement your new way of living.

PERSPECTIVE

This shift in perspective is essentially the exercise for this chapter. So do not take this light heartedly. What's great about this shift in perspective is that you can use it for just about anything. Whenever fear arises and you step out of your comfort zone you will be able to look through this lens as if you're putting on a pair of sunglasses to block the sun from beaming into your eyes. To successfully implement a change in behaviors, a change in habits, a change in lifestyle, you have to lean into this fear. I'm telling you flat out right now, it will arise. So, there is no excuse to sit there and say that you don't understand this foreign feeling. Now that you have this awareness that fear will inevitably arise from stepping out of your comfort zone, you know what you must do. It will be very difficult at first, absolutely. I will share a statement that you can say to yourself each and every day, to get over that fear. For those who know me personally, I do trade currencies in the foreign exchange market. This required me to get out of my comfort zone. I had to get used to risking my hard-earned dollars in a very volatile market. With this statement alone, it held me accountable through that process to where I've worked my fear like a muscle and made it my you know what!

"My belief and faith in myself will carry me

until my comfort catches up!"

Do not expect this to happen

overnight, because it won't. Don't expect it

to happen tomorrow. Don't even expect it to

happen next week or next month. This is an

every day ordeal. Think of it as a non-

negotiable, a standard to get over your fear

each day of living this new lifestyle that you

have created for yourself. If you come in with

no expectation, and just pure appreciation

that one day you will not fear being 100%

yourself in the face of those who think

otherwise or just in life in general, then that

day will come sooner than you think.

BRAVERY

Referring to what was discussed in the

previous chapter about conformity, think

about how many people conform to others'

beliefs based on this limited way of thinking.

It all stems from fear. Fear of being yourself.

Fear of not being *"normal "*. Fear of being

different and sharing different values and

beliefs. As you are going through this book

right now ask yourself this question, "Have I been conforming?". The majority of us have. So do not feel bad if your answer is "Yes". It is OKAY if you have conformed in the past. But it is NOT OKAY now with this new awareness to continue to conform to other people's beliefs, especially ones that you do not share.

The opposite of conformity in my eyes is bravery. It is a courageous act to be 100% yourself in this day and age. We are highly influenced by social media, the news, and the limiting beliefs that we have been taught our whole lives. So, to be anything different than what others expect you to be, is to be daring and bold. Lean into that adventurous feeling

of creating a new lifestyle and new behaviors

that serve you and don't hold you back from

your unlimited potential. My friend, you are

being 100% yourself, armed with new

standards and new values, backed by a belief

in the things that give meaning to your life;

your why, in the face of fear is audacious in

many different ways! It is the exact step

required for you to GET OVER YOURSELF!

CHAPTER 6: GET OVER YOURSELF

BEING UNCOMFORTABLE

I believe that this agitation that we feel as human beings when we feel uncomfortable really is a sign for us to move and act. More or less, it is the same when we feel hungry. It signals us to eat. We can use the same feeling or signal to overcome ourselves in the face of adversity. This adversity I speak of will be the challenges you face when implementing these tools to GET OVER YOURSELF. There's no way around it. So, you might as well go through it, and come out on the other side as a better version of you. You have probably heard this statement many times but I'm gonna say it again, "Get comfortable with being uncomfortable." You will shock yourself if you learn how to work your comfort zone more than it works you. You will look in the mirror one day and say, "Dang who the hell is that?!" It is truly an unprecedented skill set to have to live on the edge without going too far and also not shrinking to fit your own or other's limited

beliefs.

YOU CAN CHANGE YOUR MIND

If there is anything that you learned

from this book, besides all the tools and

strategies I gave you to implement to GET

OVER YOURSELF, it is that you have the

ability to change your mind. It's okay to

change your beliefs. It's okay to change the

thoughts you think. There is nothing wrong

with that and you have the power and

potential to do that. I know this can be very

difficult to think about because so many of us

define ourselves by our past and what others have taught us our whole life. Nevertheless, I do not believe that we are defined by our past. I believe that we are defined by what we seek in our future and what we do today to get us there. The power we seek over our lives is found in the present and only you can change what you do today to find a better tomorrow. Rehearsing all destructive behaviors, limiting thoughts and beliefs will provide you with what you've already had. Therefore, it's no wonder that people firmly believe that the best way to predict their future is to look at their past. Become greater than your past and GET OVER YOURSELF.

Your future self will thank you later.

(VALUES + STANDARDS) x WHY - FEAR =   GET OVER YOURSELF

These are the steps to GET OVER YOURSELF. Operate in alignment with your standards and values because of your Why. In the face of fear and discomfort you will be able to GET OVER YOURSELF. Math is absolute. So, I thought the best way to represent this step-by-step process was to give you an equation. While I don't think this is the only way to GET OVER YOURSELF, I believe this is a great solution to putting you

on the best possible path to being the best

version of you. This is the version of you that

you can be proud of, happy to show fully to

others and most importantly hold yourself

accountable to a higher standard.

CHAPTER 7: CONCLUSION

If you actively implement all these steps into your lifestyle, you will GET OVER YOURSELF. It will not be easy doing this; but trust that on the other side is clarity in the awareness to create everlasting change. Your why is what gives meaning to your life. Remember, this is also referred to as your purpose. Life without purpose gives us no direction or vision for our future. So, go 7 Levels Deep exploring what you want out of life to figure out exactly what your why is.

Your values are going to be derived straight

from the things that give meaning to your

life. These are the beliefs that you carry

because they are important to you. There are

many different types of values such as

personal, work and character but you can

define them however you see fit. Ask yourself

"What is it that I value in my life based off of

my why?". Your standards are going to be in

direct alignment with your values. These will

be the non-negotiables in your life that you

live by as if they were law. Since you have

read this book, let's make a pact together to

<u>**never**</u> conform or adjust our boundaries to anyone or any circumstance, because that leads to conformity. Raise the bar on your standards to where your self-accountability is stronger than any other accountability others could impose upon you. Fear is expected as a result of stepping out of our comfort zone and actively implementing change into our lifestyle. Remember, this is just our brain maximizing our risk by giving us an emotion in our body to alarm us. Lean into this feeling! Your belief and faith in yourself will carry you until your comfort catches up!

Pat yourself on the back for being brave enough to take the steps to overcome yourself. Not too many people in this world believe that they can change their mind. You are taking the right steps in the right direction to stretch your comfort zone to areas you would've never thought you could. Exercising the steps all together will allow you to GET OVER YOURSELF. Once again, I would like to thank you for finishing this book and taking the first steps with me to GET OVER YOURSELF. As this is my first literary piece of work, I would love to hear your feedback as well as your stories as you go through this process. I'm very appreciative of

you for even considering this new walk of life

because it tells me that there are many more

people out there in this world just like me.

My condolences to the old version of you

because you will GET OVER YOURSELF!!!

FEEDBACK

If you made it this far in the book, THANK YOU!!! Once again, I can't stress enough how grateful I am of you to spend some of your time reading my work. I am truly blown away that someone would do that for me. If you could spare an extra minute or two, I would love to receive your feedback on the book! Whether you learned something in the book, or maybe you learned something about yourself; whatever the case maybe I would be honored to hear it! And please, be honest. This will help me become a better writer in the future, so

your contribution is duly noted. You can

reach out to me on social media

@simplecell_ on Tik Tok, Instagram and

Twitter. If you want to connect with me on

LinkedIn just search my name and I should

pop up. And I have a form specifically for the

book too so please do share here as well

since I can collect all the feedback in one

place.

https://forms.gle/ZpRJhRhApEwvGSfG8

Once again thank you for your time

and I wish you the best of luck on your

journey to GET OVER YOURSELF!